Wholeness:

A Journey Towards Mental & Emotional Healing

21-DAY DEVOTIONAL & PRAYER JOURNAL

By Amina R. Maybank

Wholeness:

A Journey Towards Mental & Emotional Healing

21-DAY DEVOTIONAL & PRAYER JOURNAL

To the One who has healed, delivered, and comforted me
To Him who loves me unconditionally
To my Constant Companion
To the One who makes me whole

Jesus.

For in Him the whole fullness of Deity (the Godhead) dwells in bodily form [completely expressing the divine essence of God]. And in Him you have been made complete [achieving spiritual stature through Christ], and he is the head over all rule and authority [of every angelic and earthly power].
Colossians 2:9-10 AMP

Note from the Author

First, thank you for taking the time to read this devotional. I'm so excited for you to understand and apply all that the Lord has given me to share with you regarding wholeness. My prayer is that God will speak to you, encourage you, and heal you as you sit with the Holy Spirit and allow Him to minister to you.

God desires for us to be whole in our minds and our emotions. However, I've noticed that many times we as Christians wear masks. We put on a façade because we feel the need to portray a certain public image. We don't want people to really know what we're going through. Sunday after Sunday we see Christians going into the House of God bound and leave out bound. We continuously see the saints of God jumping, shouting, and running in the sanctuary – but still in chains. The tragedy is, not a soul will admit that they're still struggling or unhealed in certain areas of their lives. We're shouting but our souls remain in shambles. We're running but our souls are in ruin. The enemy has used this tactic of "saving face" to keep the people of God in an unhealed state.

Most people would rather not admit that they have internal struggles or unhealed areas of their soul. Mainly because we don't want to deal with the shame or humiliation that it may cause us. However, now is the time for freedom and healing. Now is the time for deliverance. If we want to truly experience the abundant life that Christ died for us to receive, then we must be honest with ourselves and with the Holy Spirit.

Many of us have experienced some sort of pain, disappointment, trauma, and/or abuse ranging from childhood to adulthood. Unfortunately, some have yet to address these issues. These unaddressed issues and unhealed parts of us present themselves in our behavior, relationships, and our perspective on life. I want you to really indulge in this book, the scriptures, and sit with God so that He may begin to do a good work in you. I want you to be honest with God about your struggles so that you and those in your bloodline can be healed once and for all.

But He was wounded for our transgressions; He was bruised for our iniquities; The chastisement for our peace was upon Him, and by His stripes we are healed.
Isaiah 53:5

With Love,
Amina R. Maybank

Whole·ness
/ˈhōlnəs/

1. the state of forming a complete and harmonious whole; unity.
2. containing all the elements properly belonging; complete.
3. undivided; in one piece.
4. not broken, damaged, or impaired; intact. good physical or mental health.
5. uninjured or unharmed; sound.
6. a thing complete in itself or comprising all its parts or elements.
7. pertaining to all aspects of human nature, especially one's physical, intellectual, and spiritual development.

About This Journal

Wholeness: *A Journey Towards Mental and Emotional Healing* is a book designed for you to read and spend time with God. Its purpose is to lead you on a path towards healing and wholeness, a completeness in Christ.

We all have areas of our souls that need to be healed and surrendered to the Lord. My assignment is to take you on a 21-day journey with God as you address issues that you may feel uncomfortable talking about or even admitting to others. Remember, we're in this together. You are not alone. While I'm not an expert or a trained professional, the Holy Spirit is aware of your every issue and need. His understanding is infinite (Psalm 147:5) and He is the God of all comfort (2 Corinth. 1:3).

There are 21 devotionals for 21 days of reading. You may combine your reading with fasting and/or bible study. Either way, each day presents a new topic for you to explore with the Lord in the secret place of His presence.

Each day has 3 different sections: a devotional, bible verses to remember & apply, and a daily affirmation. At the end of the book is a section for your notes and/or reflections. This section is for you to write down what the Lord is speaking to you or even how He is moving in your life.

Devotional: These spiritual readings are designed to help you draw closer to God and set you on a path towards wholeness in Christ.

Bible Verses to Remember & Apply: Application is everything! We must not only read the Word but apply it to our lives. Each day there are bible verses to remember and apply pertaining to that day's topic.

Daily Affirmation: At the end of every devotional is a daily affirmation to speak over yourself. These clear, positive reminder/statements are to encourage and motivate you on your journey towards mental & emotional healing – using the Word of God. Speak life!

They begged him to let the sick touch at least the fringe of his robe, and all who touched him were healed.
Matthew 14:36

Contend with what contends with you.

Table of Contents

Note from the Author 7

About This Journal.. 10

Day 1: Confront to Conquer... 15

Day 2: The God Who Sees You.. 19

Day 3: Emotional Stability 23

Day 4: Cancel Codependency.. 27

Day 5: Positive Thoughts 31

Day 6: Armor Against Anxiety.. 35

Day 7: Defeating Depression... 39

Day 8: Saved From Suicide 43

Day 9: Childhood Trauma... 47

Day 10: Abandonment & Rejection.................................. 51

Day 11: Anger Management 55

Day 12: "T" is For Therapy.. 59

Day 13: Dysfunction From Disappointment.................... 63

Day 14: Balm for the Brokenhearted 67

Day 15: The Prince of Peace.. 71

Day 16: Purified from Pettiness 75

Day 17: Forgiveness is for You 79

Day 18: Self-Love & Self-Care 83

Day 19: Self-Esteem & Self-Worth 87

Day 20: Joy Vs Happiness 91

Day 21: Whole in Christ 95

Final Words 103

About the Author 105

References 107

Day 1
Confront to Conquer

Day 1
Confront to Conquer

et's be honest, we all have issues. We've all had our experiences with pain and had to deal with the trauma from that pain. For many, these issues and experiences have left them in a paralytic state – physically, emotionally, mentally, and spiritually. It's not the will of God that you remain in an immobile condition, never moving forward. God wants to restore health to you and heal your wounds (Jer. 30:17). He desires to heal you from every pain and deliver you from every issue associated with the trauma of your past. However, you will never conquer what you're not willing to confront.

You may have been abused, neglected, or even felt the sting of abandonment and rejection. You may be suffering from anxiety, depression, or even thoughts of suicide. The voices of insecurity and self-doubt in your mind may be getting louder and louder. But alas, you will never get your breakthrough because you continue to deny what God desires for you to defeat.

We have to be honest with ourselves and with God about what ails us. He already knows your issues and desires to help you (Is. 41:13). But you must get to the point where you don't allow shame or the opinions of others to keep you from experiencing the blessing of freedom that God has for you. Confront every spirit that the enemy is using to keep you bound. By faith get before God, pour out your heart, and be honest with Him about your pain. Thus, shall come your deliverance. According to your faith, so shall it be done for you (Matt. 9:29).

Day 1

BIBLE VERSES TO REMEMBER & APPLY:

Romans 8:37 † Yet amid all these things we are more than conquerors *and* gain a surpassing victory through Him Who loved us (Amplified, Classic Edition).

Revelation 3:21 † He who overcomes (is victorious), I will grant him to sit beside Me on My throne, as I Myself overcame (was victorious) and sat down beside My Father on His throne [Amplified, Classic Edition].

Philippians 4:13 † I have strength for all things in Christ Who empowers me [I am ready for anything and equal to anything through Him Who infuses inner strength into me; I am self-sufficient in Christ's sufficiency [Amplified, Classic Edition].

1 John 5:4† For everyone born of God is victorious *and* overcomes the world; and this is the victory that has conquered *and* overcome the world—our (continuing, persistent) faith (in Jesus the Son of God) [Amplified].

DAILY AFFIRMATION:

I am more than a conqueror and I can do all things through Christ who strengthens me.

Day 2
The God Who Sees You

Day 2
The God Who Sees You

El Roi – *The God Who Sees* is what Hagar named God after He spoke to her in Genesis chapter 16. Hagar was thrust into a situation that she didn't ask for nor sought to be a part of. Yet here she was misunderstood, alone, and pregnant – and no one truly saw her except God.

Your circumstances or dysfunction may not have come by your own hand. Maybe it was your parents, a past lover, or a friend that you trusted. Regardless of how you got to this place, know that you serve a God who sees you. He sees beyond your actions – He sees the why. He sees beyond your faults and flaws – He sees the pain. He knows your making and that you are but dust (Psalm 103:14). When there is no one to turn to and you feel alone, God is there with open ears and an open heart ready to receive you. He's seen every heartbreak, every disappointment, and every traumatic experience you've endured. Nothing you bring to God in prayer will take Him by surprise.

Wholeness begins when we recognize that the God of the bible is the same yesterday, today, and forever (Heb. 13:8). It begins when we cast our cares on Him knowing that He cares for us (1 Peter 5:7). He's able to bring you out to a steady place – a place of peace. El Roi is able to make your feet like hinds' feet and set you upon high places (Ps. 18:33). Be confident when you pray, knowing that the same God who hears you sees you, and wants to make you into all that He's created you to be. Behold, the eye of the Lord is on those who fear Him, on those who hope in His steadfast love (Psalm 33:18).

Day 2

BIBLE VERSES TO REMEMBER & APPLY:

Job 34:21 † For [God's] eyes are upon the ways of a man, and He sees all his steps [Amplified, Classic Edition].

Jeremiah 23:24 † Can anyone hide himself in secret places so that I cannot see him? says the Lord. Do not I fill heaven and earth? says the Lord [Amplified, Classic Edition].

Psalm 33:13 † The Lord looks down from heaven and sees every person [New Century Version].

1 Samuel 16:7 † But the Lord said to Samuel, Look not on his appearance or at the height of his stature, for I have rejected him. For the Lord sees not as man sees; for man looks

on the outward appearance, but the Lord looks on the heart [Amplified, Classic Edition].

DAILY AFFIRMATION:

God looks down from heaven and His eyes are upon me. He sees my heart and is acquainted with all my ways. The God of the universe sees me.

Day 3
Emotional Stability

Day 3
Emotional Stability

It's not the will of God that we live in a state of emotional instability. It's not His will that our emotions be all over the place – happy one minute, sad the next. God gave us emotions, but He desires for us to control our emotions and not allow our emotions to control us. Proverbs 25:28 warns us that a man without self-control is like a city broken into and left without walls. Sometimes, we can't control what happens to us or how people treat us. Nevertheless, we can control how we react to our circumstances and mistreatment from others.

He who is slow to anger is better than the mighty, and he who rules his spirit than he who captures a city (Prov. 16:32). There is a supernatural strength in self-control. One of the fruits of the Spirit is self-control. We have the Spirit of God in us, so that means we can do all things through Christ who strengthens us (Phil. 4:13). We can control our emotions. We can have emotional stability. It's up to us to ask the Lord to enable us to do so.

Have you ever seen a person with a hot temper or whose mood depends on the day? It's unhealthy and it's not a good look. Emotional instability can make a fully grown adult look like an immature toddler. Apart of being a whole and healthy person is learning to control your emotions. God desires for His people to be healthy. Ask the Holy Spirit to enable you to control your emotions. He's able.

Day 3

BIBLE VERSES TO REMEMBER & APPLY:

Proverbs 4:23 † Keep and guard your heart with all vigilance and above all that you guard, for out of it flow the springs of life (Amplified, Classic Edition).

Colossians 3:15 † Let the peace of Christ [the inner calm of one who walks daily with Him] be the controlling factor in your hearts [deciding and settling questions that arise]. To this peace indeed you were called as members in one body [of believers]. And be thankful (to God always) [Amplified].

2 Timothy 1:7 † For God did not give us a spirit of timidity or cowardice or fear, but [He has given us a spirit] of power and of love and of sound judgment and personal discipline [abilities that result in a calm, well-balanced mind, and self-control] [Amplified].

1 Thessalonians 4:4 † For everyone born of God is victorious and overcomes the world; and this is the victory that has conquered and overcome the world—our (continuing, persistent) faith (in Jesus the Son of God) [Amplified].

DAILY AFFIRMATION:

I have the Holy Spirit and my character yields fruit of the Spirit. Therefore, I have self-control. I control my emotions; my emotions don't control me.

Day 4
Cancel Codependency

Day 4
Cancel Codependency

"Codependency can be defined as any relationship in which two people become so invested in each other that they can't function independently anymore...your mood, happiness, and identity are defined by the other person..." (Gilbert et al., 2020). Let me say, if you are depending on anyone other than Jesus Christ for your happiness, mood, and/or identity – you are headed for a grave disappointment. Your self-worth is found in your identity in Jesus Christ, not your relationships.

God the Father is your Creator. He's the One who gives you your identity and your purpose. Genesis 1:27 says, "So God created man in His own image, in the image of God He created him; male and female He created them." Your spouse, children, parents, friends, mentor, etc. shouldn't be a crutch that you lean on for your identity. You are who God says you are. Proverbs 20:7-8 says, "Some trust in chariots, others in horses, but we trust the Lord our God. They are overwhelmed and defeated, but we march forward and win." People change. However, God does not (Malachi 3:6). No matter who comes and who goes,

Christ is the only constant in your life. Everything and everyone else are secondary, an addition to your life.

When we look to people to give us peace and purpose, we put them in the place of Almighty God. Only God can provide the peace that surpasses all human understanding (Phil. 4:7). By God's providence, the people in your life can be a means of support, happiness, and love. Nonetheless, the Lord is your Source. It is the Creator that we worship not the creature. Depend on God for your value, not people.

Day 4

BIBLE VERSES TO REMEMBER & APPLY:

Psalm 20:7 † Some trust in chariots, and some in horses; But we will remember the name of the Lord our God (New King James Version).

Proverbs 29:25 † The fear of man brings a snare, but whoever leans on, trusts in, and puts his confidence in the Lord is safe and set on high [Amplified, Classic Edition].

Proverbs 3:5 † Lean on, trust in, and be confident in the Lord with all your heart and mind and do not rely on your own insight or understanding [Amplified, Classic Edition].

Psalm 118:8 † It is better to trust and take refuge in the Lord than to put confidence in man [Amplified, Classic Edition].

DAILY AFFIRMATION:

I am not ensnared because I take refuge in the Lord. I trust in the Lord with all my heart, and I don't lean on my own understanding.

Day 5
Positive Thoughts

Day 5
Positive Thoughts

Most of our battles begin in the mind. It is the battlefield where the enemy attacks God's people. Guarding your thoughts and thinking positively can make a huge difference in how you behave and relate to others. Your thoughts can either hinder or help you, discourage or encourage you, paralyze or propel you.

In Philippians 4:8, The Apostle Paul tells us to think on those things that are true, honest, just, pure, lovely, things of a good report, virtuous and praiseworthy. Thinking negatively about yourself and your circumstances produces negative feelings. It affects your mood, your joy, and even your faith. This is usually the place where depression and anxiety begin. You must set your mind on things above (heavenly matters), not earthly things (Colossians 3:2). Get in the habit of thinking about what you're thinking about. Ponder your thoughts, choose your thoughts, be selective in what you think...*casting down imaginations, and every high thing that exalts itself against the knowledge of God, and bringing into captivity every thought to the obedience of Christ* (2 Cor. 10:5).

Spend time in God's presence. Think on His goodness, faithfulness, and the answered prayers that you've received. Praise Him for what He's already done in your life. Praise gives way to a thankful heart – which is a result of thinking on things that are true, praiseworthy, and of a good report. You must dedicate time specifically for spending time with God through prayer and reading His Word to renew your mind. Let the Holy Spirit change your way of thinking and *be continually renewed in the spirit of your mind [having a fresh, untarnished mental and spiritual attitude]* (Ephesians 4:23).

Day 5

BIBLE VERSES TO REMEMBER & APPLY:

Philippians 4:8 † Finally, believers, whatever is true, whatever is honorable and worthy of respect, whatever is right *and* confirmed by God's word, whatever is pure *and* wholesome, whatever is lovely *and* brings peace, whatever is admirable *and* of good repute; if there is any excellence, if there is anything worthy of praise, think *continually* on these things (center your mind on them, and implant them in your heart) [Amplified].

Colossians 3:2 † Set your mind and keep focused habitually on the things above (the heavenly things), not on things that are on the earth which have only temporal value [Amplified].

2 Corinthians 10:5 † casting down arguments and every high thing that exalts itself against the knowledge of God, bringing every thought into captivity to the obedience of Christ... [New King James Version].

Romans 8:5-6 † For those who are living according to the flesh set their minds on the things of the flesh [which gratify the body], but those who are living according to the Spirit, [set their minds on] the things of the Spirit (His will and purpose). Now the mind of the flesh is death (both now and forever—because it pursues sin); but the mind of the Spirit is life and peace [the spiritual well-being that comes from walking with God—both now and forever) [Amplified].

DAILY AFFIRMATION:

I have life and peace because my mind is governed by the Spirit of God. I set my mind on things above, not on earthly things.

Day 6
Armor Against Anxiety

Day 6
Armor Against Anxiety

To be anxious is to worry, to feel uneasy and nervous about something with an uncertain outcome. The cares of this world is enough to make one anxious. However, the bible is clear about the cure for anxiety. In Matthew 6:33, God tells us to "seek first the Kingdom of God and all His righteousness and everything else will be added to us." This means we are to focus on God's way of doing things and being right, making Him the 1st priority in our lives. He promised to supply all our needs according to His riches and glory in Christ Jesus (Phil 4:19). Our Heavenly Father has promised to take care of us, so why do we worry? We worry because we don't trust Him enough to fulfill His promises and because we're looking at what we see.

The Word tells us to be anxious for nothing, but in every situation, by prayer and supplication, with thanksgiving, make our requests known to God, and the peace of God that transcends all human understanding will guard our hearts and minds in Christ Jesus (Phil 4:6-7).

Armor against anxiety with The Word (your sword) and put your trust in God knowing that He will perfect those things that concern you (Ps. 138:8). Trust that He sees, hears, and knows you. Now is not the time to worry, but to put your faith into action. Pray and keep praying knowing that God Almighty is sovereign. He's in control of your circumstances.

"Fear not, for I am with you; be not dismayed, for I am your God; I will strengthen you, I will help you, I will uphold you with my righteous right hand." Isaiah 41:10

Day 6

BIBLE VERSES TO REMEMBER & APPLY:

Philippians 4:6 † Do not fret or have any anxiety about anything, but in every circumstance and in everything, by prayer and petition ([a]definite requests), with thanksgiving, continue to make your wants known to God [Amplified, Classic Edition].

1 Peter 5:7 † Casting the [a]whole of your care [all your anxieties, all your worries, all your concerns, [b]once and for all] on Him, for He cares for you affectionately and cares about you [c]watchfully [Amplified, Classic Edition].

John 14:1 † Do not let your hearts be troubled (distressed, agitated). You believe in and adhere to and trust in and rely on

God; believe in and adhere to and trust in and rely also on Me [Amplified, Classic Edition].

Psalm 94:19 † In the multitude of my [anxious] thoughts within me, Your comforts cheer and delight my soul! [Amplified, Classic Edition]

DAILY AFFIRMATION:

I am not anxious for anything because I make my requests known unto God by prayer and supplication with thanksgiving. The peace of God that transcends all human understanding guards my heart and mind in Christ Jesus.

Day 7
Defeating Depression

Day 7
Defeating Depression

There were several people in the Bible who were depressed. One person who stands out is King David. This was a man after God's own heart and a mighty warrior who suffered from depression from time to time. In one verse he would be praising God and the next he's saying, "I am worn out from sobbing. All night I flood my bed with weeping, drenching it with my tears. My vision is blurred by grief..." (Ps. 6:6). David was unable to sleep because he was so overwhelmed with sadness, and he cried all night. How many nights have you had like this?

Even though David was depressed, he learned how to come out of it. He learned how to encourage himself. He often put on a garment of praise for the spirit of heaviness. We don't realize that our praise is a weapon. I know that it's hard to praise God when your eyes are flooded with tears and the answers to your prayers seem afar off. But David said, "I will bless the Lord at all times, His praises shall continually be in my mouth" (Ps. 34:1). He understood the power of praise.

2 Chron. 20:22 explains, "at the very moment they began to sing and give praise, the Lord caused the armies of Ammon, Moab, and Mount Seir to start fighting among themselves." God will cause your praise to confound the enemy of your soul.

Choose to believe God by faith and praise your way through the battle. While your praising, seek the professional help you need as well. In the multitude of counsel, there is safety (Prov. 11:14).

Lift up your heads, O you gates; and be lifted up, you age-abiding doors, that the King of Glory may come in. Who is this King of Glory? The Lord strong and mighty, the Lord mighty in battle. (Ps. 24:7)

Day 7

BIBLE VERSES TO REMEMBER & APPLY:

Matthew 11:28 † Come to Me, all you who labor and are heavy-laden and overburdened, and I will cause you to rest. (I will [a]ease and relieve and [b]refresh [c]your souls) [Amplified, Classic Edition].

Psalm 55:22 † Cast your burden on the Lord (releasing the weight of it) and He will sustain you; He will never allow the (consistently) righteous to be moved (made to slip, fall, or fail) [Amplified, Classic Edition].

Psalm 9:9 † The Lord also will be a refuge and a high tower for the oppressed, a refuge and a stronghold in times of trouble (high cost, destitution, and desperation). [Amplified, Classic Edition].

Nehemiah 8:10 † Then he said to them, "Go your way, eat the fat, drink the sweet, and send portions to those for whom nothing is prepared; for this day is holy to our Lord. Do not sorrow, for the joy of the Lord is your strength" [New King James Version].

DAILY AFFIRMATION:

As I cast my burden on the Lord, He will sustain me. The Lord is my refuge and a stronghold for me in times of trouble.

Day 8
Saved From Suicide

Day 8
Saved From Suicide

Your life matters. Your testimony matters. You matter. Your life is so precious and is so meaningful to God, that He sent His only Son to die on the cross for your sins (John 3:16). The enemy would love nothing more than to plant lies in your head that would tell you the opposite. God has a plan for your life and it's the enemy's job to see to it that you don't believe this truth. He wants you to give up hope, give up on God, and live in a place of hopelessness. After all, the thief's job is to steal, kill, and destroy. However, Christ came that you might have life, and have it more abundantly – to the full (John 10:10).

The battle starts in the mind and that's where the enemy plants seeds of doubt, unbelief, and lies. No matter what God allows you to face in life - He is good and He is present. I know at times this may be difficult to believe, but it's true. Believe it by faith. He said that He would never leave nor forsake you (Hebr. 13:5) The Lord is with you in your present circumstances, I don't care how bad it looks. It's not the will of God for you take your own life. He's able to turn any situation around and work it out for your good.

You're not forgotten. There is more life for you to live. Don't allow the enemy to trick you into thinking your life is over or that it's better if you take your own life. God created you for a purpose. He had a goal in mind when He created you. You're not a mistake and you are on the mind of God. Precious are God's thoughts towards you. So much so that they can't be numbered (Ps. 139:17).

Those who choose suicide (for whatever reason) should remember that death is not the end, but a doorway into an eternal existence. Sad to say, some who find the pain of dying intolerable will awaken in a realm that is even more terrible than earth could ever be. We should welcome death from the hand of God, but not force the hand that brings it. - Erwin Lutzer

Day 8

BIBLE VERSES TO REMEMBER & APPLY:

2 Corinthians 4:8-9 † We are hedged in (pressed) on every side [troubled and oppressed in every way], but not cramped or crushed; we suffer embarrassments and are perplexed and unable to find a way out, but not driven to despair; We are pursued (persecuted and hard driven), but not deserted [to stand alone]; we are struck down to the ground, but never struck out and destroyed; [Amplified, Classic Edition].

Psalm 42:11 † Why are you cast down, O my soul? And why are you disquieted within me? Hope in God; For I shall yet praise Him, The help of my countenance and my God [New King James Version].

John 16:33 † I have told you these things, so that in Me you may have [perfect] peace and confidence. In the world you have tribulation and trials and distress and frustration; but be of good cheer [take courage; be confident, certain, undaunted]! For I have overcome the world. [I have deprived it of power to harm you and have conquered it for you.] [Amplified, Classic Edition].

John 10:10 † The thief comes only in order to steal and kill and destroy. I came that they may have and enjoy life, and have it in abundance (to the full, till it [a]overflows) [Amplified, Classic Edition].

DAILY AFFIRMATION:

I will not allow the enemy to steal, kill, or destroy my life as I have abundant life in Christ Jesus. God has purpose and a plan for my life.

Day 9
Childhood Trauma

Day 9
Childhood Trauma

According to Northwestern University Feinberg School of Medicine, child trauma refers to a scary, dangerous, violent, or life-threatening event that happens to a child (0-18 years of age). An event can be traumatic when we face or witness an immediate threat to ourselves or to a loved one, and it is often followed by serious injury or harm. So many of us, especially those of us who grew up in less than fortunate circumstances experienced some sort of childhood trauma. Many of us didn't get the help that we needed because of lack of finances and/or lack of understanding of the long term effects of unresolved childhood trauma.

Thanks be to God, there is Good News! 2 Corinthians 5:17 tells us, "If any man be in Christ, he is a new creature: old things are passed away; behold, all things are become new." The old things have passed away and we are new in Christ. Childhood trauma can leave one brokenhearted and wounded in their souls. Nevertheless, Psalms 147:3 says, "He heals the brokenhearted and binds up all their wounds." Hallelujah! You are not a victim of your past or any childhood trauma that you've experienced. Christ died to set you free. If the Son sets you free, you are free indeed. (John 8:36).

Almighty God is a Deliverer and He's able to heal all your wounds. However, don't neglect the ministry of counseling and therapy. The Lord knows that there is healing in talking about our issues. Thus, He's given us professional therapists and counselors. There is healing for the inner child in you. There's deliverance for that deep seeded hurt that you've been carrying around for years. God says, "I will compensate you for the years that the locust hath eaten, the cankerworm, and the caterpillar, and the palmerworm, my great army which I sent among you" (Joel 2:25).

Day 9

BIBLE VERSES TO REMEMBER & APPLY:

2 Corinthians 5:17 † Therefore if any person is [ingrafted] in Christ (the Messiah) he is a new creation (a new creature altogether); the old [previous moral and spiritual condition] has passed away. Behold, the fresh and new has come! [Amplified, Classic Edition].

John 8:36 † So if the Son makes you free, then you are unquestionably free [Amplified].

Psalm 147:3 † He heals the brokenhearted and binds up their wounds (healing their pain and comforting their sorrow) [Amplified, Classic Edition].

Joel 2:25 † "And I will compensate you for the years that the swarming locust has eaten, the creeping locust, the stripping locust, and the gnawing locust—My great army which I sent among you" [Amplified].

DAILY AFFIRMATION:

I am not a victim of my past. I am in Christ. Therefore, I am a new creature: old things have passed away; behold I have become new.

Day 10
Abandonment & Rejection

Day 10
Abandonment & Rejection

A bandonment and rejection sneak their way into our lives in various ways. Whether it be through childhood neglect, friends walking away, a spouse leaving – the results are the same: people choosing to leave our lives. Rejection can make you feel less than and cause you to question your worth when someone that you love walks away. You may even feel unloved and unwanted. The truth is, sometimes God will allow people to leave us to show us that He is our Source of all things that we need. His love and presence in our lives is constant. He never leaves.

When a person chooses to leave your life, rejoice. The people who are connected to your God-given purpose must stay and those who aren't must leave. In the book of Ruth, we see two women (Orpah and Ruth) in the same situation (death of their husbands) with a choice to either stay or go. The difference between the two women is only one chose to stay with their mother-in-law, Naomi who served the one true and living God. (Ruth 1:8-14). The other left because her part of the journey was over. Later on, we see the Lord's purpose for Ruth and

Naomi as Ruth became a great descendent of our Lord Jesus Christ.

The Psalmist in Psalms 142:4-5 says, *Look to the right and see: there is none who takes notice of me; no refuge remains to me; no one cares for my soul. I cry to you, O Lord; I say, 'You are my refuge, my portion in the land of the living.* You may feel the sting of loneliness, the hurt of abandonment, and the soreness from rejection; but the Lord is with you. God will never leave nor forsake you. Reach out to Him, He's present.

Day 10

BIBLE VERSES TO REMEMBER & APPLY:

Psalm 27:10 † Although my father and my mother have forsaken me, yet the Lord will take me up [adopt me as His child]. [Amplified, Classic Edition].

Isaiah 49:15-16 † [The Lord answered] "Can a woman forget her nursing child, And have no compassion on the son of her womb? Even these may forget, but I will not forget you. Indeed, I have inscribed [a picture of] you on the palms of My hands; Your city walls [Zion] are continually before Me" [Amplified].

Psalm 142:4-5 † Look on my right hand and see, for there is no one who acknowledges me; Refuge has failed me; No one cares for my soul. I cried out to You, O Lord: I said, "You are my refuge, My portion in the land of the living [New King James Version].

1 Peter 2:4 † "Come to Him [then, to that] Living Stone which men [a]tried and threw away, but which is chosen [and] precious in God's sight. [Amplified].

DAILY AFFIRMATION:

If my mother and father forsake me, the Lord will take me in. He will never leave nor forsake me.

Day 11
Anger Management

Day 11
Anger Management

Self-control is a fruit of the Spirit (Gal. 5:23). If you can't control your anger, you are bound for trouble – trouble with your friends, family, colleagues, and eventually the law. Only a fool gives vent to his spirit, but a wise man quietly holds it back (Prov 29:11). It's not a sin to be angry. Jesus was angry. In John 2:14, Jesus was so angry that he started flipping over tables! However, this was a righteous or holy indignation as Jesus saw the house of God being used as a marketplace. On the other hand, there is an anger that will cause you to harm others and yourself. There's nothing wrong with being angry. The problem occurs when one doesn't know how to manage it.

Have you ever seen a toddler throw a tantrum because he or she couldn't have their way? Or an immature teen become extremely angry because he lost a game? Likewise, have you ever seen an adult man or woman become so angry that they lose all self-control: shouting, yelling, throwing things, and causing a scene? Looks quite foolish and immature, doesn't it? A man of wrath stirs up strife, and one given to anger causes much transgression (Prov. 29:22). When a person loses their temper and can't control it, their liable to do or say anything. This can be dangerous.

Apart of being healthy and whole is learning how to manage your emotions, including anger. God wants us to rule our emotions, not our emotions to rule us. There's nothing worse than an angry, mean, and bitter Christian. Seek the Lord in His word about anger management and seek counseling if you feel you need additional help.

Day 11

BIBLE VERSES TO REMEMBER & APPLY:

Ecclesiastes 7:9 † Do not be eager in your heart to be angry, For anger dwells in the heart of fools. [Amplified].

Proverbs 15:18 † A hot-tempered man stirs up strife, but he who is slow to anger appeases contention. [Amplified, Classic Edition].

Ephesians 4:26 † Be angry [at sin—at immorality, at injustice, at ungodly behavior], yet do not sin; do not let your anger (cause you shame, nor allow it to) last until the sun goes down [Amplified].

James 1:20 † For man's anger does not promote the righteousness God (wishes and requires). [Amplified, Classic Edition].

DAILY AFFIRMATION:

I am not easily provoked in my spirit. Anger dwells in the heart of fools, and I am not a fool.

Day 12
"T" is For Therapy

Day 12
"T" is For Therapy

I've never seen anywhere in the bible where Jesus was opposed to professional help. With prayer and therapy, I believe that we can reach the wholeness in Christ that God wants for us. For some, all it takes is prayer and fasting. For others, wholeness may mean adding therapy to the equation. Too many of God's people are walking around in shackles because they refuse to get the professional help that they need. Proverbs 11:14 tells us where there is no guidance, a people fall, but in an abundance of counselors there is safety. If you need to talk to someone about your issues, then do so!

Therapy is the treatment of mental or psychological disorders by psychological means. Countless people are suffering in their minds but refuse to get help because of what others may think. However, God is a God of wisdom. Of course, we need to pray and fast. The scripture talks about "this kind" only comes out by prayer and fasting (Matt. 17:21). Only you know what your "this kind" is – however, continue to seek the professional help that you need so that you may be healed in Jesus' name. There are some things in life that we must go the extra mile for and our emotional & mental health are some of those things. Some people have suffered repeated trauma since childhood and devastating disappointments that haven't been addressed or healed. Then, they bring those unhealed parts of themselves into relationships as adults. This is not healthy.

Proverbs 24:6 says, "for by wisdom you can wage your war, and in abundance of counselors there is victory". Whatever tactic that the enemy has used to wage war against your mind, your will, and emotions, fight back! Fight back with prayer, fasting, and therapy. It feels good to unload and vent to others. Why not do it with a trained professional?

Day 12

BIBLE VERSES TO REMEMBER & APPLY:

Proverbs 12:15 † The way of the [arrogant] fool [who rejects God's wisdom] is right in his own eyes, But a wise and prudent man is he who listens to counsel [Amplified].

Proverbs 11:14 † Where there is no [wise, intelligent] guidance, the people fall [and go off course like a ship without a helm], But in the abundance of [wise and godly] counselors there is victory [Amplified].

Proverbs 15:22 † Without consultation and wise advice, plans are frustrated, But with many counselors they are established and succeed [Amplified].

Proverbs 24:6 † For by wise counsel you can wage your war, and in an abundance of counselors there is victory and safety [Amplified, Classic Edition].

DAILY AFFIRMATION:

I will win every emotional and mental battle as I seek the Lord and heed wise, godly counsel.

Day 13
Dysfunction From Disappointment

Day 13
Dysfunction From Disappointment

Disappointment happens to us all. The crushing of a dream not realized, a desire not met, an expectation or hope not fulfilled can leave one devastated. Psalm 13:12 says, "Hope deferred makes the heart sick, but when desire is fulfilled, it is a tree of life." As a result of experiencing one disappointment after another, some people become dysfunctional in the way they think, act, or feel. To grasp a better understanding of what it means to be dysfunctional, some synonyms for the word dysfunctional are: flawed, broken, debilitated, defective, sick, and wounded. The damage caused by continuous disappointment can leave one broken, debilitated, and wounded to the point where all hope seems lost.

Maybe you don't believe that anything good will ever happen to you. Perhaps, you no longer trust that God's promises will ever come to pass in your life. Take courage, God wants you to hope again. Have faith in God's love for you and His faithful character. I know it's easier said than done, but God is able to fulfill the desires of your heart. You may be weary from believing God at this point. Nevertheless, "He gives power to the faint, and to him who has no might, He increases strength. Even the youths shall grow weary, and young men shall fall exhausted; but they who wait for the Lord shall renew their strength; they shall mount up with wings like eagles; they shall run and not be weary; they shall walk and not faint." (Isaiah 40:29-31). All you need is a mustard seed of faith (Matt 17:20). Believe again.

Day 13

BIBLE VERSES TO REMEMBER & APPLY:

Romans 5:5 † Such hope [in God's promises] never disappoints us, because God's love has been abundantly poured out within our hearts through the Holy Spirit who was given to us. [Amplified].

Proverbs 16:9 † A man's mind plans his way (as he journeys through life), But the Lord directs his steps and establishes them. [Amplified].

Psalm 34:5 † They looked to Him and were radiant; Their faces will never blush in shame or confusion. [Amplified].

Proverbs 19:21 † Many plans are in a man's mind, But it is the Lord's purpose for him that will stand (be carried out) [Amplified].

DAILY AFFIRMATION:

As I look to the Lord for help, I will not be put to shame. Many are the plans in my heart, but the Lord's purpose will prevail in my life.

Day 14
Balm for the Brokenhearted

Day 14
Balm for the Brokenhearted

The "Balm of Gilead" is a rare perfume that is used medicinally. This particular balm is used as a good herbal treatment for curing headaches and is also a great remedy for various skin problems, cuts, wounds, burns and many other medical conditions. In general, it's used as a healing agent for the body. In Jeremiah 46:11, the Prophet Jeremiah told God's people, "Go up to Gilead and obtain [healing] balm, O Virgin Daughter of Egypt! In vain you use many medicines; For you there is no healing or remedy." In other words, the people had used every kind of medicine they could for healing – but to no avail.

Many people turn to prescription & recreational drugs, alcohol, sex, money, etc. to heal their heartache. However, Jesus is the only balm you need to heal your broken heart. He's the Great Physician. Whether your heart is broken due to a divorce, loss of a loved one, or a great disappointment – the Lord can heal your heart. He can heal your wounds if you let Him. Psalm 147:3 declares, "He heals the brokenhearted and binds up all their wounds."

Turn to Him in prayer – cry aloud, spare not, and lift up your voice. He can handle your weeping and your frustrations. He's able to cure the brokenness you feel in your soul. The Lord is close to the brokenhearted and saves those who are crushed in spirit (Psalm 34:18). Jesus is your balm.

Day 14

BIBLE VERSES TO REMEMBER & APPLY:

Psalm 34:18-19 †The Lord is close to those who are of a broken heart and saves such as are crushed with sorrow for sin and are humbly and thoroughly penitent. Many evils confront the [consistently] righteous, but the Lord delivers him out of them all [Amplified, Classic Edition].

Psalm 147:3 † He heals the brokenhearted and binds up their wounds (curing their pains and their sorrows) [Amplified, Classic Edition].

Revelation 21:4 † and He will wipe away every tear from their eyes; and there will no longer be death; there will no longer be sorrow and anguish, or crying, or pain; for the [a]former order of things has passed away [Amplified].

1 Peter 4:19 † Therefore, those who are ill-treated and suffer in accordance with the will of God must [continue to] do right and commit their souls [for safe-keeping] to the faithful Creator [Amplified].

DAILY AFFIRMATION:
The Lord continually heals any brokenness in my heart and binds up all my wounds.

Day 15
The Prince of Peace

Day 15
The Prince of Peace

Life and all its cares can make us feel overwhelmed and heavy if we allow it. Many people literally lose their minds focusing on their problems instead of the Problem Solver. The bible tells us that He will keep him in perfect peace whose mind is stayed on Him, because he trusts in Him (Is. 26:3). You have to make it a constant habit to keep your mind on Jesus. Not that you ignore your problems, but you focus on the One who can solve your problems and can lift your heavy burdens.

The word peace is defined as *1. freedom from agitation or disturbance by the passions, as from fear, terror, anger, anxiety, or the like; quietness of mind; tranquility; calmness; quiet of conscience. 2. Heavenly rest; the happiness of heaven.* Anything or anyone that is a detriment to your peace, you need to let go. It is not the will of God that you live in anxiety, depression, and worry about anything. Philippians 4:6-7 tells us to be anxious for nothing, but in everything by prayer and supplication with thanksgiving, let our requests be made known to God. He promises that the peace of God that surpasses all human understanding will guard our hearts and minds through Christ Jesus. Peace is your portion.

The thief (satan) comes only to steal, kill, and destroy (John 10:10). His job is to destroy, steal, and kill your peace by any means necessary. He does this by planting negative thoughts in your mind, telling you lies that are not cohesive with the word of God, causing you to doubt God's faithfulness. The devil is a liar. You shall have peace!

Jesus can keep your mind in perfect peace despite what is going on in your life and in the world around you. It is the will of God for you to live in perfect peace. Turn your problems over to Him. Keep your mind on Him and His promises. Be still and know that He is God (Ps. 46:10).

Day 15

BIBLE VERSES TO REMEMBER & APPLY:

John 14:27 † Peace I leave with you; My [own] peace I now give and bequeath to you. Not as the world gives do I give to you. Do not let your hearts be troubled, neither let them be afraid. (Stop allowing yourselves to be agitated and disturbed; and do not permit yourselves to be fearful and intimidated and cowardly and unsettled) [Amplified, Classic Edition].

Psalm 23:2 † He makes me lie down in (fresh, tender) green pastures; He leads me beside the still and restful waters. [Amplified, Classic Edition].

2 Thessalonians 3:16 † Now may the Lord of peace Himself grant you His peace (the peace of His kingdom) at all times and in all ways [under all circumstances and conditions, whatever comes]. The Lord [be] with you all. [Amplified, Classic Edition].

Isaiah 26:3 † You will guard him and keep him in perfect and constant peace whose mind [both its inclination and its character] is stayed on You, because he commits himself to You, leans on You, and hopes confidently in You. [Amplified, Classic Edition].

DAILY AFFIRMATION:

The Lord always gives me peace in every way. I am in perfect peace because I keep my mind stayed on Him.

Day 16
Purified from Pettiness

Day 16
Purified from Pettiness

To be petty is to be childish, simply put. You can't be powerful and be petty – the two don't mix. However, we've all been there – someone says or does something to intentionally hurt or irritate us, and we feel the need to respond in a negative, nasty, or childish way. Wisdom says that you don't need to respond in anger, wrath, or retaliate. Friend, good sense makes one slow to anger, and it is his glory to overlook an offense (Prov. 19:11). We must learn to be the bigger person, the better person, the godly person. After all, if we don't, then are we truly mature in Christ?

God wants us mature, not childish. 1 Corinth. 13:11 says, "When I was a child, I spoke as a child, I understood as a child, I thought as a child: but when I became a man, I put away childish things." In that same chapter, the writer is talking about what genuine love truly is and looks like. Pettiness is not love. It's easier to respond in our flesh and vindicate ourselves. But Romans 12:19, reminds us not to avenge ourselves, but leave it to the wrath of God, for it is written, "Vengeance is mine, I will repay, says the Lord."

We have to trust that God will deal with those who oppose us. We must become mature enough to ignore insults. You're not responsible for how others treat you. However, you're accountable to God for how you treat others. To be powerful is to be able to ignore the temptation to be petty. We are not petty people; we are powerful people. How can you grow in Christ with a petty mindset and a petty attitude? You can't be "Petty Pam" or "Petty Pete" and claim maturity in Christ. It doesn't work that way, Beloved. God is watching to see if you will repay evil for evil or good for evil. I know it's hard, but allow the Holy Spirit to purify you from pettiness and ask for His help to ignore the pettiness of others.

Day 16

BIBLE VERSES TO REMEMBER & APPLY:

Proverbs 19:11 † Good sense makes a man restrain his anger, and it is his glory to overlook a transgression or an offense [Amplified, Classic Edition].

Proverbs 15:1 † A soft and gentle and thoughtful answer turns away wrath, But harsh and painful and careless words stir up anger [Amplified].

Romans 12:18 † If it is possible, as much as depends on you, live peaceably with all men [Amplified, Classic Edition].

Hebrews 12:14 † Strive to live in peace with everybody and pursue that consecration and holiness without which no one will [ever] see the Lord [Amplified, Classic Edition].

DAILY AFFIRMATION:

I overlook offenses. I strive to live peaceably with all men. Vengeance belongs to the Lord.

Day 17
Forgiveness is for You

Day 17
Forgiveness Is for You

We've all been hurt or wronged by someone. Likewise, we've all done something to hurt or offend others. It happens. The problem occurs when we hold on to negative feelings and remain bitter and angry towards the one who caused the offense. You may think you're hurting them by remaining angry, but in reality, you're hurting yourself.

There are various researches that have been carried out which shows that unforgiveness causes health issues including: **cancer** – 61% of cancer patients have forgiveness issues, **suppressed anger** – people often get angry for any reason have issues associated with forgiveness, **low self-esteem** – lack of self-love stem from not forgiving yourself or self-acceptance, **bitterness** – increases the risk of depression, constant worrying increases of the risk **sleep deprivation and anxiety**, **high blood pressure,** and **heart disease** (Megase, 2019). The consequences of living in bitterness and unforgiveness cost you more than the other person.

Forgiveness doesn't mean that you don't acknowledge the other person's wrong doing. Rather you choose to let it go. It doesn't give your offender a free pass. However, it does free you from the crippling effect of unforgiveness and releases the other person to God.

God calls us to forgive as He forgives us. Think of the many trespasses and sins you've committed against God with your thoughts, words, and actions. Yet, He is faithful and just to forgive you and cleanse you from all unrighteousness (1 John 1:9). He does not deal with us according to our sins, nor repay us according to our iniquities (Psalm 103:10). Release yourself from the chains of bitterness and live in the freedom to which Christ has called you.

Day 17

BIBLE VERSES TO REMEMBER & APPLY:

John 14:27 † Peace I leave with you; My [own] peace I now give and bequeath to you. Not as the world gives do I give to you. Do not let your hearts be troubled, neither let them be afraid. (Stop allowing yourselves to be agitated and disturbed; and do not permit yourselves to be fearful and intimidated and cowardly and unsettled) [Amplified, Classic Edition].

Psalm 23:2 † He makes me lie down in (fresh, tender) green pastures; He leads me beside the still and restful waters. [Amplified, Classic Edition].

2 Thessalonians 3:16 † Now may the Lord of peace Himself grant you His peace (the peace of His kingdom) at all times and in all ways [under all circumstances and conditions, whatever comes]. The Lord [be] with you all. [Amplified, Classic Edition].

Isaiah 26:3 † You will guard him and keep him in perfect and constant peace whose mind [both its inclination and its character] is stayed on You, because he commits himself to You, leans on You, and hopes confidently in You. [Amplified, Classic Edition].

DAILY AFFIRMATION:

I choose to forgive myself and those who have wronged me. I am free from the bondage of unforgiveness and bitterness.

Day 18
Self-Love & Self-Care

Day 18
Self-Love & Self-Care

Self-care is a form of self-love. You don't mistreat someone that you love, right? So why would you mistreat or mishandle yourself. How you treat yourself, take care of yourself, and even speak to yourself exposes how you truly feel about you. God commands us to love our neighbor as we love ourselves (Mark 12:31). Aside from loving our neighbor, it's imperative that we love ourselves as God loves us. In order to love ourselves and extend that same love to others, we must fully understand God's love for us. His love for us is without condition. He loves us no matter what – nothing can separate us from the love of God (Romans 8:39).

What you put in your body, how you maintain your body, how you talk to yourself, all matters to God. It should matter to you as well. Taking time for yourself, maintaining your body, making sure that you have peace of mind is all part of self-care. If you don't take care of you, then who will? Take some time to meditate on God's love for you. In turn, take some time to love on yourself today.

God loves you and He wants you to love yourself. Knowing God is knowing love, as God is love (1 John 4:8). The more acquainted you become with God, the more you will love Him and yourself. As a result, you'll be more equipped to love others as you have the love of God flowing in your heart.

Love brings you face to face with yourself. It's impossible to love another if you cannot love yourself. – John Pierrakos

Day 18

BIBLE VERSES TO REMEMBER & APPLY:

1 Corinthians 6:19-20 † Do you not know that your body is the temple (the very sanctuary) of the Holy Spirit Who lives within you, Whom you have received [as a Gift] from God? You are not your own, You were bought with a price [purchased with a preciousness and paid for, [c]made His own]. So then, honor God and bring glory to Him in your body [Amplified, Classic Edition].

1 Corinthians 3:16 † Do you not discern and understand that you [the whole church at Corinth] are God's temple (His sanctuary), and that God's Spirit has His permanent dwelling in you [to be at home in you, [a]collectively as a church and also individually]? [Amplified, Classic Edition].

Romans 12:1 † I appeal to you therefore, brethren, and beg of you in view of [all] the mercies of God, to make a decisive dedication of your bodies [presenting all your members and faculties] as a living sacrifice, holy (devoted, consecrated) and well pleasing to God, which is your reasonable (rational, intelligent) service and spiritual worship [Amplified, Classic Edition].

1 John 4:19 † We love Him because He first loved us [New King James Version].

DAILY AFFIRMATION:

I put on love. I love myself and others as God is love.

Day 19
Self-Esteem & Self-Worth

Day 19
Self-Esteem & Self-Worth

Self-esteem is a widely used concept both in popular language and in psychology. A number of factors can negatively influence one's self esteem: childhood neglect, abusive relationships, worldly views, rejection, and so forth. However, God intends for you to see yourself the way that He sees you.

Psalm 139:13-14 says, "For you created my inmost being; you knit me together in my mother's womb. I praise you because I am fearfully and wonderfully made; your works are wonderful; I know that full well." You are God's masterpiece...a wonderful work. God created you the way that you are on purpose. Every detail was carefully crafted by your Heavenly Father. He created you in His own image (Gen. 1:26).

1 Peter 2:9 declares, "you are a chosen race, a royal priesthood, a holy nation, a people for His own possession..." You are royal because God says so. Don't allow mistreatment and the opinions of others to make you think otherwise. When you know your worth, you won't settle for anything less than

God's best for your life. When you value yourself, you won't allow anyone to mishandle you. You're valuable to God and His Kingdom. You're so valuable that He sent His only begotten Son to die for your sins. You are of great value to the Lord. Know that your worth and esteem comes from God, your Creator. Your identity is found in Christ alone.

Day 19

BIBLE VERSES TO REMEMBER & APPLY:

Psalm 139:14 † I will give thanks and praise to You, for I am fearfully and wonderfully made; Wonderful are Your works, And my soul knows it very well. [Amplified].

Genesis 1:27 † So God created man in His own image, in the image and likeness of God He created him; male and female He created them [Amplified, Classic Edition].

1 Peter 2:9 † But you are a chosen race, a royal priesthood, a consecrated nation, a [special] people for God's own possession, so that you may proclaim the excellencies [the wonderful deeds and virtues and perfections] of Him who called you out of darkness into His marvelous light [Amplified].

Isaiah 43:4 † "Because you are precious in My sight, You are honored and I love you..." [Amplified].

DAILY AFFIRMATION:

I am fearfully and wonderfully made; I was created in the image of God, the Creator of the universe.

Day 20
Joy Vs Happiness

Day 20
Joy Vs Happiness

*A*ll hell can be breaking loose in your life, but you can still have a smile on your face. That smile isn't there because everything is perfect. It's there because you know that "all things are working together for your good" (Rom. 8:28). In the midst of heartache, pain, disappointment, etc. God is able to make you smile. He's able to fill your mouth with laughter and your lips with shouting (Job 8:21).

There is a difference between joy and happiness. Joy is deeply rooted. It's an internal feeling that isn't dependent upon external factors. Nehemiah 8:10 says, *The joy of the Lord is our strength* and Psalm 16:11 tells us that, *In His presence is fullness of joy.* We when enter into the presence of the Lord through praise, worship, prayer...we're able to access His joy and His peace that surpasses all understanding. Joy can't be taken away by people or the things happening around us.

Happiness is indeed a great feeling. However, happiness is dependent upon external circumstances. It's circumstantial. It doesn't go beyond the surface of what we see. Happiness changes just like the people and situations around us. It's not constant...but the joy of the Lord is...because He is constant. You can choose how you feel. You can choose your mood. You don't have to wait until your circumstances change to experience joy, laughter, and God's peace. Seek His presence and experience His joy for yourself.

It's your choice...choose joy.

Day 20

BIBLE VERSES TO REMEMBER & APPLY:

Psalm 34:8 † I will give thanks and praise to You, for I am fearfully and wonderfully made; Wonderful are Your works, And my soul knows it very well. [Amplified].

Psalm 16:11 † So God created man in His own image, in the image and likeness of God He created him; male and female He created them [Amplified, Classic Edition].

Nehemiah 8:10 † But you are a chosen race, a royal priesthood, a consecrated nation, a [special] people for God's own possession, so that you may proclaim the excellencies (the wonderful deeds and virtues and perfections) of Him who called you out of darkness into His marvelous light [New King James Version].

John 15:11 † I have told you these things so that My joy and delight may be in you, and that your joy may be made full and complete and overflowing [Amplified].

DAILY AFFIRMATION:

The joy of the Lord is my strength. I don't depend on my temporal circumstances to determine my mood.

Day 21
Whole in Christ

Day 21
Whole in Christ

Jesus healed the bleeding woman in the Gospels (Matt. 9:20-22, Mark 5:25-34, Luke 8:43-48). This unnamed woman was bleeding for 12 long years. She desperately tried every physician and spent all of her money for 12 years in search of healing but to no avail. There was only One who could heal her. But alas, it was her faith that made her whole. Jesus said to her, "Daughter, your faith has cured you. Go in peace and be whole from your disease" (Mark 5:34). Your faith is the key that will unlock your healing and deliverance. Your faith is what will make you whole.

Without faith, it's impossible to please God. He who comes to God must believe that He exists and that He is a rewarder of those who diligently seek Him (Heb. 11:6). Wholeness comes from trusting God. It comes from knowing who your Heavenly Father is and who you are in Him. Wholeness comes when you become strong enough in the Lord to resist the devil that he may flee from you (James 4:7).

Christ has made you free. You may not feel free, but by faith speak it over your life, cry out to the Lord, get the professional & spiritual help that you need...and walk in your victory. For in Him the whole fullness of deity dwells bodily, and you have been filled in him, who is the head of all rule and authority (Col. 2:9-10). Those of us who are saved have the Spirit of Jesus living on the inside of us. The same power that resurrected Jesus Christ from the dead is living on the inside of you. You can live again. You can do all things through Christ who strengthens you (Phil. 4:13). Those areas of your life, character, and soul that need healing, God can do it. You can't do it on your own or in your own strength. However, with God all things are possible. Wholeness is your portion.

Day 21

BIBLE VERSES TO REMEMBER & APPLY:

Colossians 2:9-10 † For in Him the whole fullness of Deity (the Godhead) continues to dwell in bodily form [giving complete expression of the divine nature]. And you are in Him, made full and having come to fullness of life (in Christ you too are filled with the Godhead—Father, Son and Holy Spirit—and reach full spiritual stature). And He is the Head of all rule and authority (of every angelic principality and power) [Amplified].

Mark 5:34 † Then He said to her, "Daughter, your faith [your personal trust and confidence in Me] has restored you to health; go in peace and be [permanently] healed from your suffering" [Amplified].

1 Thessalonians 5:23 † Now may the God of peace Himself sanctify you through and through [that is, separate you from profane and vulgar things, make you pure and whole and undamaged—consecrated to Him—set apart for His purpose]; and may your spirit and soul and body be kept complete and [be found] blameless at the coming of our Lord Jesus Christ [Amplified].

2 Peter 1:3 † as His divine power has given to us all things that pertain to life and godliness, through the knowledge of Him who called us by glory and virtue [New King James Version].

DAILY AFFIRMATION:

By His divine power, God has given me everything that I need that pertains to life and godliness. I am whole in Christ Jesus.

Reflections and Notes

_____

_____

_____

_____

_____

_____

_____

_____

_____

_____

_____

_____

_____

_____

_____

_____

_____

_____

_____

_____

_____

_____

_____

_____

Final Words

God wants you whole and He wants you healed. One of the benefits of being a Child of God is that you partake in the blessing of the Lord which makes you rich and add no sorrow (Proverbs 10:22). Rich doesn't necessarily refer to finances. It means your overall quality of life. Furthermore, healing is a benefit of the Lord's blessing. God says in 3 John 1:2, Beloved, I pray that you may prosper in all things and be in health, just as your soul prospers. It is His will that you prosper. By faith, believe and receive this for yourself. Whether it be mental, emotional, or physical – your health matters to God. You matter to God.

When we come to Christ, we are to put on the "new man" as it says in Ephesians 4:24. God understands that before you gave your life to Him, you experienced trauma, pain, and for some abuse. Likewise, even as a saved, Spirit filled Christian, we all have baggage that He desires for us to lay at His feet. Some of us still have things that we need deliverance from even after years of serving God. My prayer is that as you continue to seek the Lord for healing and wholeness in your soul, you will allow Him to expose and repair the areas of your heart, personality, mind, and emotions that the enemy has damaged over the years. God is able.

We all can have accidents in life. God knew this, and so He sent Jesus as our Healer. His healing touch is God's mercy to us. If you are hurt, ask God to heal you and then trust Him to do it in His way and in His time. - Stormie O'martian

About the Author

orn and raised in Newark, NJ, Amina relocated to Philadelphia, PA in 2009 as she answered the call of God for a new life in Christ. Amina is a licensed minister, author, and encourager. She has served as a faithful member at Brand New Life Christian Center in Philadelphia, PA for the past 13 years operating in leadership roles for various ministries such as the Singles Ministry, Young Adult Ministry, and the Intercessory Team.

An aspiring writer since an adolescent, Amina has fulfilled her lifelong dream of becoming a published author through Words From Heaven Publishing in which she is the founder and CEO. In 2014, Amina published her 1st book entitled, "Single, Saved & Seeking Him" which is geared towards helping singles in the Body of Christ seek the Lord and His purpose for their lives. She also maintains *Words by Amina*, which is a faith-based blog purposed to address the topics that Christians face in their daily lives all while encouraging people to seek God's will in every circumstance.

In May 2021, Amina launched her very own Podcast, "Faith to Faith Podcast", which is purposed to encourage the hearts of God's people and win the lost for Christ, one episode at a time. Minister Amina is determined to fulfill God's purpose for her life and seeks to inspire others to do the same.

Read Amina's blog at:
www.aminaswords.blogspot.com

Listen to Amina's Podcast at:
www.anchor.fm/castthevision

References

Gilbert, B., Upham, B., Weinstock, C. P., Lindberg, S., Splitter, J., Vogt, C., Rapaport, L., & Pugle, M. (2020, July 16). *Do you have a codependent personality?* EverydayHealth.com. Retrieved from https://www.everydayhealth.com/emotional-health/do-you-have-a-codependent-personality.aspx.

Megase, K. (2019, December 29). Unforgiveness and your health. Counselling Directory. Retrieved from https://www.counselling-directory.org.uk/memberarticles/unforgiveness-and-your-health

What is child trauma? Center for Child Trauma Assessment and Service Planning. (2020, June 22). Retrieved from http://cctasi.northwestern.edu/child-trauma/.

www.ingramcontent.com/pod-product-compliance
Lightning Source LLC
Chambersburg PA
CBHW051841040426
42447CB00006B/643